Contents

About the story

Robert Louis Stevenson wrote many novels. He began *Treasure Island* in 1881 to entertain his stepson while they were staying in Scotland. It was published in 1883. He said that it was written as an experiment – a 'boys' adventure story' which was 'silly and horrid fun!' At first he planned to call it *The Sea Cook or Treasure Island: A Story for Boys*.

He wrote to a friend telling him that one problem was having to be careful about the oaths (swearing) that the pirates used. After all, parents as well as boys would read it!

In this book, there are secrets, murder plots, fights, deaths, and of course treasure! As you read the book, find reasons why it might have been called *The Sea Cook*. Nowadays, is it really a boys' adventure or have times changed? Does it appeal to girls as well?

Characters in the story

Jim Hawkins
The young hero who tells the story
of the adventure to find the treasure.

Billy Bones
The pirate Captain who
had the treasure map.

Black Dog and Blind Pew
Two pirates who visit Billy Bones to get the map.

Doctor Livesey
Jim's friend who joins
him on the sea journey.

Squire Trelawney
The man who buys the ship
to set sail for the treasure.

Captain Smollett
The Captain of the ship.
A sensible man.

Long John Silver
A one-legged pirate who is
a natural leader of men.

Israel Hands
A pirate who tried to
murder Jim, but got
killed instead.

George Merry
A pirate and a
trouble-maker.

Ben Gunn
A sailor who was left all
alone on Treasure Island.

Abraham Gray
A loyal and honest sailor.

Tom Redruth
One of the Squire's
servants who is killed
by the pirates.

Mr Dance
A customs officer who
helps Jim take the map
safely to the Squire.

Jim Hawkins begins his story. He tells us about a frightening old sea-captain who comes to stay at his father's inn.

I go back to the time when my father kept the 'Admiral Benbow' inn, and the old seaman took up his lodging under our roof.

I remember him as he came to the inn door, his sea-chest behind him in a hand-barrow. He was a tall, strong man with a **sabre** cut across one cheek.

He rapped on the door and called roughly for rum.

This is a handy **cove**. Much company, mate?

No, very little, the more the pity.

Well, then this is the **berth** for me. I'll stay here a bit.

He was a very silent man. All day he hung round the cove, or upon the cliffs, with a brass telescope. All evening he sat next to the fire and drank rum.

sabre – a long curved sword   **cove** – a small bay   **berth** – a place where a ship docks

1

Every day, when he came back from his stroll, he would ask if any seafaring men had gone by. At first, we thought it was the want of company of his own kind, but we began to see he **was desirous** to avoid them.

He promised me a silver fourpenny on the first of every month if I would keep my eyes open for a seafaring man with one leg and let him know the moment he appeared.

There were nights when he took a deal more rum than his head would carry; and then he would sing his wicked old sea-songs.

His stories frightened people. Dreadful stories they were: about hanging, walking the plank, storms and wild deeds. He must have lived his life among some of the wickedest men that God ever allowed upon the sea.

Fifteen men on a dead man's chest – Yo-ho-ho, and a bottle of rum! Drink and the devil had done for the rest – Yo-ho-ho, and a bottle of rum!

was desirous – wanted to

An evil man called Black Dog visits the Captain and makes him so angry he has a stroke! But he tells Jim something very strange. Sadly, Jim's father dies.

It was a bitter cold winter. My poor father **was little likely to see the spring**.

One January morning, the Captain had risen earlier than usual and set out down the beach. Mother was upstairs with father.

The door opened and a man stepped in.

Is this here a table for my mate Bill? He has a cut on one cheek.

You and me'll get behind the door and give Bill a little surprise.

At last in strode the Captain and marched across the room to his breakfast.

Bill.

The Captain spun round. He had the look of a man who sees a ghost.

Black Dog!

Come for to see his old shipmate.

Speak up: what is it?

We'll sit down and talk like old shipmates.

was little likely to see the spring – would probably be dead by spring

For a long time I could hear nothing. At last the voices began to grow higher. All of a sudden there was a tremendous explosion of **oaths**, a clash of steel, a cry of pain and I saw Black Dog in full flight.

Jim, rum! I must get away from here!

I ran to fetch it, but I heard a loud fall in the parlour, and running in, beheld the Captain lying full length upon the floor. He was breathing very hard and loud; but his eyes were closed and his face was a horrible colour.

The door opened and Dr Livesey came in, on his visit to my father.

oaths – swearing

Where is he wounded?

No more wounded than you or I. This man has had a stroke.

4

settle him – finish him off   peach – tell

Another evil-looking man, Blind Pew, calls on the Captain and causes his death!

So things passed until three o'clock of a foggy frosty afternoon. I saw someone along the road. He was blind. I never saw a more dreadful looking figure.

I hear a young voice. Will you give me your hand, and lead me in?

Take me in to the captain, or I'll break your arm.

When I'm in view, cry out, 'Here's a friend for you, Bill.'

I cried out the words.

Bill, sit where you are.

Jim and his mother are scared that Black Dog and Blind Pew might come back. Nobody will help them, so they take what the Captain owes them and run off ...
... just in time ...

It occurred to us to seek help in the **hamlet**. The more we told of our troubles, the more they clung to the shelter of their houses. The name of Captain Flint carried a great weight of terror. Not one would help us to defend the inn.

Back we will go.

We set forth in the cold night.

We found the key and hurried upstairs.

His box was like any other seaman's chest. We found nothing of value but the silver and the trinkets, a bundle tied up in **oilcloth** and the jingle of gold.

My mother began to count. I heard the tapping of the blind man's stick. We could hear the bolt rattling. Then there was silence. A little low whistle sounded a good way off upon the hill.

I'll take what I have.

And I'll take this oilskin packet.

hamlet – small village   **oilcloth** – waterproof material

8

We opened the door and were **in full retreat**. The sound of several footsteps running came to our ears.

We were just at the little bridge, so there we had to stay within earshot of the inn.

My enemies began to arrive.

Down with the door!

Bill's dead!

Search him. Is it there?

The money's there.

Flint's fist, I mean.

We don't see it here!

It's these people of the inn – find 'em.

Just then, the whistle, but this time twice repeated. It was a signal to warn them of approaching danger.

in full retreat – running away

doubloons – Spanish gold coins   buccaneers – pirates

The oilskin package turns out to contain a map showing where Captain Flint's treasure is! The Squire decides to get hold of a ship and they will all sail for this treasure.

Dr Livesey had gone up to the Hall to dine with the Squire. The servant showed us into a great library. Mr Dance told his story.

Jim, you have the thing that they were after, have you?

You have heard of this Flint, I suppose?

He was the bloodthirstiest buccaneer that sailed.

Supposing that I have here some clue to where Flint buried his treasure.

If we have the clue, I fit out a ship in Bristol dock, take you and Hawkins along. I'll have that treasure if I search a year.

The paper had been sealed. The doctor opened the seals and there fell out the map of an island.

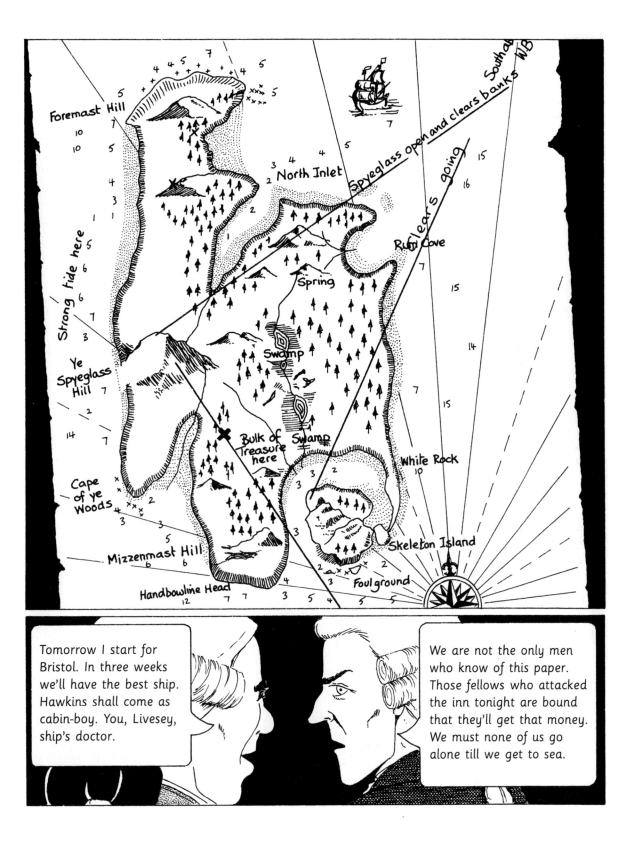

Tomorrow I start for Bristol. In three weeks we'll have the best ship. Hawkins shall come as cabin-boy. You, Livesey, ship's doctor.

We are not the only men who know of this paper. Those fellows who attacked the inn tonight are bound that they'll get that money. We must none of us go alone till we get to sea.

A letter arrives from the Squire and Jim sets off for the ship.

So the weeks passed till one fine day there came a letter.

Old Anchor Inn, Bristol.

The ship is bought and fitted ready for sea, name 'Hispaniola'. My old friend Blandly **slaved in my interest**, so did everyone in Bristol as soon as they got wind we sailed for treasure. I was standing on the dock when I fell in talk with an old sailor. I **engaged** him to be ship's cook. Long John Silver! He has lost a leg. We put together the toughest old **salts**.

Come full speed to Bristol, John Trelawney

The **mail** picked us up at the 'Royal George'. I must have slept like a log. When I was awakened the day had already broken.

Where are we?

Bristol.

We met Squire Trelawney.

Oh sir, when do we sail?

Tomorrow!

slaved in my interest – worked hard for me   **engaged** – employed   **salts** – sailors   **mail** – coach

Jim meets Long John Silver and spots Black Dog. He isn't sure whether to trust Silver.

The Squire gave me a note addressed to Silver. I had taken a fear that he might be the one-legged sailor.

Mr Silver, sir?

Oh, I see. You are our new cabin-boy.

One of the customers suddenly made for the door.

Stop him! It's Black Dog!

Run and catch him.

My suspicions reawakened on finding Black Dog at the 'Spy-glass'. I watched the cook narrowly. Two men had come back and confessed they had lost the track.

Here's a hard thing. Trelawney, what's he to think? I let him give us all the slip.

Now, Hawkins, you do me justice with the Cap'n.

On our little walk he made himself the most interesting companion. I began to see that here was one of the best shipmates.

My suspicions reawakened – I was suspicious again

When we got to the inn, Long John told the story. We all agreed there was nothing to be done.

All hands aboard by four this afternoon.

Captain Smollett doesn't like the look of the crew or the way they are organising the ship. He thinks there could be trouble.

hands – sailors   mutiny – take over

The ship sets sail and Jim hears a frightening conversation.

'The Hispaniola' begun her voyage to the Isle of Treasure.

Every man on board seemed well content. Double **grog** was going on the least excuse, **duff** on odd days and always a barrel of apples.

It was about the last day of our outward voyage. I was on my way to my berth, it occurred to me that I should like an apple.

grog – rum and water   **duff** – pudding

I got into the apple barrel, and found there was scarce an apple left.

A heavy man sat down close by. I was just about to jump up when the man began to speak. It was Silver's voice. I lay there and I understood that the lives of all the honest men aboard depended upon me alone.

Now here's what I say. You'll live hard and speak soft till I give the word.

What I say is, when? That's what I say.

I'll tell you when. The last moment I can manage; and that's when. We can steer a course, but who's to **set one**? Cap'n Smollett.

Wait, but when the time comes, let her rip! I claim Trelawney. I'll wring his head off his body.

Fancy the terror I was in! Yet I gathered some important news.

Not another man'll **jine**.

There were still faithful men on board.

Just then the voice of the look-out shouted.

Land ho!

set one – work out where to sail **jine** – join

19

They see Treasure Island. Jim tells the Squire, Captain Smollett and the doctor about the conversation he heard. They make plans. When they drop anchor, Jim decides to go ashore.

We saw two low hills and rising behind one of them, a third hill.

Has any one of you ever seen that land ahead?

I have sir.

I have a chart here. See if that's the place.

Yes sir. This is the spot to be sure.

Captain Smollett, the Squire and Dr Livesey were talking. I **durst** not interrupt them openly.

Doctor. Get to the cabin. Send for me. I have terrible news.

My lads. You'll have grog served out for you to drink!

durst – dared

20

The three gentlemen went below. Word was sent that Jim Hawkins was wanted in the cabin. I told the whole details of Silver's conversation.

You were right. I await your orders.

We must go on. We have time before us. There are faithful hands. I propose to **come to blows** when they least expect it.

We can count on your own servants?

As upon myself.

Three, ourselves make seven.

Only seven out of the twenty-six on whom we could rely.

We must keep a look-out till we **know our men**.

come to blows – fight   **know our men** – know who's on our side

We brought up about a third of a mile from either shore, the mainland on one side and Skeleton Island on the other.

The men became truly threatening, growling together in talk. Mutiny hung over us like a thunder-cloud.

Let's allow the men an afternoon ashore. If they all go, we'll fight the ship. If none go, we hold the cabin. If some go, Silver'll bring 'em aboard as mild as lambs.

My lads. A turn ashore'll hurt nobody.

They gave a cheer.

Six fellows were to stay on board. Our party could not fight the ship.

I slipped over the side in the nearest boat. Silver, from the other boat, called out to know if it were me.

The crews raced for the beach; but the boat I was in shot far ahead.

I caught a branch and swung myself out.

Jim, Jim!

I paid no heed. I ran till I could run no longer.

Jim witnesses a murder and meets Ben Gunn. He tells Jim how he came to be left alone on the island.

I began to look around the strange island.

I came to a thicket of oak-like trees. Soon I heard voices. Crawling, I made towards them.

Silver, you're honest or I'm mistook. Will you be led away with that **mess of swabs**?

All of a sudden — one horrid scream

What was that?

That? Oh, I reckon that'll be Alan.

You've killed Alan have you? Kill me too if you can.

It struck Tom. Like enough, his back was broken.

Silver buried his knife twice in that defenceless body.

mess of swabs – evil group of sailors

I began to crawl back. I ran and, as I ran, fear grew and grew upon me. There was nothing left but death.

I saw a figure leap behind the trunk of a pine.

I had heard of cannibals. But he was a man, however wild. I stood still. My pistol flashed into my mind. Courage glowed in my heart. I walked towards him.

Who are you?

Ben Gunn. I haven't spoke with a Christian these three years.

You mightn't happen to have a piece of cheese about you? I've dreamed of cheese!

If ever I get aboard again, you shall have cheese!

If ever you get aboard, says you. I'm rich. Now tell me true, that ain't Flint's ship?

25

The doctor goes ashore. He finds the **stockade**. He, the Squire, Captain Smollett and the loyal men decide to leave 'The Hispaniola' and hole up in the stockade with arms and supplies. He thinks Jim is dead.

Narrative continued by the doctor. Hunter came down with the news that Jim had slipped into a boat and gone ashore. It was decided that Hunter and I should go ashore with the **jolly-boat**.

I had not gone a hundred yards when I came on the stockade.

There came the cry of a man at the point of death.

Jim Hawkins is gone!

Aboard the schooner, I told my plan to the Captain. We fell to loading the boat. Pork, powder and biscuit. We were clear out of the ship but not yet in our stockade.

stockade – land surrounded by a fence   **narrative** – story   **jolly-boat –** small boat

They lose their supplies when their boat sinks. They reach the stockade, losing a man. The pirates steal their goods from the sunken boat, but Jim turns up safe!

The one danger was the gun.

The boat sank. There were all our stores at the bottom. Only two guns remained in a state for service. We waded ashore leaving the jolly-boat and half of our powder and provisions.

We came to the stockade and, almost at the same time, seven mutineers appeared.

Redruth stumbled and fell. We laid him in the log house to die.

The captain had run up the **colours**.

A shot passed the roof. The second ball descended in the stockade.

Captain, it must be the flag they are aiming at. Would it be wiser to take it in?

No, sir.

The ebb has made a good while; our stores should be uncovered.

Grey and Hunter stole out but the mutineers were busy carrying off our stores. Silver was in command.

I was wondering over poor Jim Hawkins's fate.

Doctor, Squire, Captain, hullo!

colours – Union Jack   **The ebb … good while** – The tide must be out by now

Jim tells them about Ben Gunn and how they reached the stockade. Long John Silver turns up. He demands the treasure map. When he doesn't get it, he tells them they'll all die.

As soon as Ben Gunn saw the colours he came to a halt.

There's your friends sure enough. Silver would fly the **Jolly Roger**.

When Ben Gunn is wanted you know where to find him.

I lay for some time watching the **bustle**. Then I skirted the woods and was soon warmly welcomed by the faithful party. I told my story.

Is this Ben Gunn a man?

I am not sure whether he's sane.

A man who has been three years biting his nails on a desert island can't expect to appear sane. Was it cheese he had a fancy for? In my box I carry a piece. That's for Ben Gunn.

I was dead tired and I slept like a log. I was awakened by the sound of voices.

Silver himself!

Jolly Roger – pirate flag **bustle** – action

to **Davy Jones** – drown

The pirates attack the stockade, but Jim and his friends win the fight!

Before the hour's out we shall be **boarded**.

An hour passed.

Suddenly a rifle-ball knocked the Doctor's musket into bits.

Pirates swarmed over the stockade like monkeys.

Shots were fired. The log-house was full of smoke.

boarded – attacked

The fight was over, the victory was ours. Hunter lay stunned, Joyce shot through the head never to move again.

The Captain's wounded.

Have they run?

There's five will never run again.

Five against three leaves us four to nine. That's better odds than we had.

Jim finds Ben Gunn's boat. He decides to cut 'The Hispaniola' loose and let it drift. Something goes wrong!

There was no return of the mutineers. Hunter never recovered. After dinner the doctor set off through the trees.

He's going to see Ben Gunn.

As for the scheme I had – I was to find the white rock and **ascertain whether** it was there Ben Gunn had hidden his boat.

I took my way to go down the sea side. I walked along the surf.

I found the boat, but I had taken another **notion** . . . to cut 'The Hispaniola' adrift and let her go ashore where she fancied.

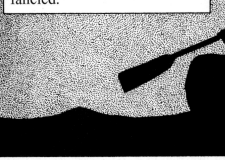

ascertain whether – find out if   **notion** – idea

There lay 'The Hispaniola'.

I felt the **hawser** slacken in my grasp.

I cut one strand after another until the vessel only swung by two.

I felt the hawser slacken once more and cut the last fibre. My hands came across a cord. I grasped it. I pulled in hand over hand on the cord.

I got my eye above the window-sill. Israel Hands and his companion locked together in a wrestle, each with his hand upon the other's throat.

Suddenly, the schooner gave a violent **yaw**. One shout followed another. I could hear feet pounding. I lay down in the bottom of that **skiff** and **recommended my spirit to its Maker**.

hawser – anchor rope **yaw** – movement off course **skiff** – (Ben Gunn's) small boat
recommended ... Maker – prayed to God to take care of me

Jim spends a terrifying night at sea in Ben Gunn's little boat. He manages to board 'The Hispaniola'. One man is dead and Israel Hands is wounded. Hands says he'll help Jim to anchor the ship.

It was day when I woke and found myself at the south-west end of Treasure Island. I sat up to try paddling.

Right in front of me I beheld 'The Hispaniola'. It became plain to me that nobody was steering. Where were the men?

Suppose she was deserted? If not, the men were lying drunk below where I might **batten them down** perhaps, and do what I chose with the ship.

I sprang to my feet, caught the jib-boom. I clung there panting.

The schooner charged down and struck the **coracle**. I was left without retreat on 'The Hispaniola'.

batten them down – lock them in   **coracle** – Ben Gunn's boat

strike 'em – take them down

The breeze served us admirably – the coast of the island flashing by. I was pleased with the bright weather . . .

. . . but the **coxswain** watched, and watched and watched me at my work.

We sat in silence over another meal.

Jim, get me a bottle of wine.

He wanted me to leave the deck.

I scuttled down, ran quietly and popped my head out of the **fore companion**. His leg hurt him yet he trailed across the deck, picked out a long knife and trundled back again.

We both desired a sheltered place and until that was done my life would be certainly spared.

coxswain – one who steers a ship   **fore companion** – door to the front cabins

Israel Hands attacks Jim. 'The Hispaniola' runs aground and Jim kills the pirate.

We had two miles to run. We dodged in. 'The Hispaniola' ran on for the wooded shore.

Steady – **starboard** – **larboard** a little – steady.

When I looked round, there was Hands half way towards me.

He threw himself forward. I leaped sideways.

I drew a pistol ...

... neither flash nor sound. I had no time to use my other pistol.

Suddenly 'The Hispaniola' ground in the sand.

starboard – to the right **larboard** – to the left

I sprang into the **mizzen shrouds** and did not draw breath till I was seated on the cross-trees. I lost no time in changing the priming of my pistol.

Hands began slowly and painfully to mount.

One more step, Mr Hands, and I'll blow your brains out.

Back went his right hand over his shoulder. I felt a blow and I was pinned by the shoulder to the mast.

My pistols went off.

The coxswain plunged headfirst into the water.

He was dead.

mizzen shrouds – ropes attached to the mast

Jim leaves the ship. He goes back to the stockade but the pirates are already there.

I did what I could for my wound. I let myself drop softly overboard. The sun went down. I began to set my face for the **blockhouse** and my companions. The night fell blacker; the moon was climbing higher. I came down upon the clearing.

As I drew nearer it was like music to hear my friends snoring peaceful in their sleep. My foot struck a sleeper's leg.

Pieces of eight!

Silver's green parrot, Captain Flint!

I turned to run. Arms held me tight.

Bring me a torch, Dick!

So, here's Jim Hawkins, dropped in like, eh?

Pieces of eight – Spanish silver coins
blockhouse – a house made of logs

Jim's friends have left. The pirates want Jim dead, but Silver is not too sure – the pirates get angry.

There were six of the buccaneers.

Jim, I see you were smart when first I set my eyes on you. Now Jim, you can't go back to your own lot for they won't have you; you'll have to jine with Cap'n Silver.

I have a right to know where my friends are.

They've **tramped**. I don't know where's they are.

Kill me or spare me. One thing I'll say: if you spare me **bygones are bygones** and when you fellows are in court for piracy I'll save you all I can.

We've split upon Jim Hawkins.

Then here goes!

Avast there! I never seen a better boy than that. He's more a man than any pair of rats of you!

tramped – walked off   **bygones are bygones** – we'll forgive and forget   **we've split upon** – we've had enough of

42

swinging – hanging

Dr Livesey comes to the stockade. He speaks to Jim and gives Silver a warning!

I was wakened by a clear voice.

Here's the Doctor.

He entered the blockhouse and with one grim nod to me proceeded with his work among the sick.

I should wish to talk with that boy, please.

Step outside o' that stockade. I'll bring the boy down on the inside. You can **yarn** through the **spars**.

You make a note of this – how I saved his life. You'll **speak me fair**. I step aside and leave you and Jim alone.

Jim, we'll run for it.

No, I passed my word.

yarn –talk   spars – posts   speak me fair – put in a good word for me

Jim and the pirates set off to look for the treasure. They find a very unusual compass!

We made a curious figure all in **soiled** sailor clothes, all but me armed to the teeth. I had a line about my waist like a dancing bear.

There was some discussion on the chart and the note on the back.

Tall tree, Spy-glass Shoulder. Skeleton Island. Ten feet.

The party spread itself, shouting and leaping.

The man the farthest left began to cry aloud, as if in terror.

He can't 'a' found the treasure.

soiled – dirty

When we reached the spot, a human skeleton lay on the ground.

What sort of a way is that for bones to lie?

I've a notion. Here's the compass. Take a bearing.

I thought so; this here is a **p'inter**. Right up there is our line.

Flint. This is one of his jokes, and no mistake. Him and six was alone here; he killed 'em, and this one he hauled here and laid down by compass. If Flint was living, this would be a hot spot for you and me.

He's dead, but if ever **sperrit** walked it would be Flint.

Stow this talk. He's dead and he don't walk.

The pirates kept side by side. The terror of the dead buccaneer had fallen on their spirits.

p'inter – pointer **sperrit** – spirit

The pirates are scared by a voice, but then carry on to find the buried treasure – except it has gone!

All of a sudden a voice struck up.

Fifteen men on a dead man's chest – *Yo-ho-ho*, and a bottle of rum!

It's Flint!

It's someone flesh and blood.

Darby M'Graw! Fetch the rum, Darby!

They was his last words.

I never was feared of Flint in his life. I'll face him dead.

Don't cross a sperrit.

Sperrit? No man ever seen a sperrit with a shadow. What's he doing with an echo?

Come to think on it, it was like someone else's voice, it was like …

Ben Gunn!

Nobody minds Ben Gunn, dead or alive.

The tall trees were reached. The third rose nearly two hundred feet. A red column as big as a cottage. Seven hundred thousand pounds of gold lay buried below its spreading shadow.

All together!

The **foremost** broke into a run.

Suddenly we beheld them stop. A low cry arose. Silver doubled his pace; and next moment he and I had come to a dead halt.

Before us was a great **excavation**. The sides had fallen in and grass had sprouted on the bottom. The **cache** had been found and the seven hundred thousand pounds were gone.

foremost – first   **excavation** – hole   **cache** – treasure

Jim and Silver are almost killed, but the Doctor, Ben Gunn and Gray shoot two of the pirates. The others run off.

Jim, take that and stand by for trouble.

The buccaneers found a two-guinea piece.

That's your seven hundred thousand pounds is it?

They all got out upon the opposite side from Silver.

Now mates!

But just then three musket-shots flashed out.

Merry tumbled. The man with the bandage fell. The other three ran.

The Doctor, Gray and Ben Gunn joined us.

Quick, we must head 'em off the boats.

We set off.

Doctor, see there! No hurry!

We were already between them and the boats.

It's you Ben Gunn!

How do, Mr Silver.

The Doctor, as we proceeded downhill to the boats, related a story. Ben had found the treasure. He had carried it to a cave. The Doctor had gone to Silver, given him the chart. Finding that I was to be involved in the horrid disappointment, he had prepared for the mutineers.

Ben Gunn had to work upon the superstitions of his former shipmates. Gray and the Doctor were already **ambushed** before the arrival of the treasure-hunters.

ambushed – in hiding ready to attack

We reached the **gigs**, demolished one, got aboard the other.

Just inside the mouth of North Inlet what should we meet but 'The Hispaniola'.

There was little amiss. Gray was to pass the night on guard.

A gentle slope ran up from the beach to the cave.

The Squire met us.

gigs – rowing boats   **There ... amiss** – There was not much wrong with it

We all entered. I beheld great heaps of coin and bars of gold – Flint's treasure!

What a supper I had that night – salted goat, some **delicacies** and a bottle of wine. And Silver joining in our laughter.

delicacies – tasty snacks

At last, they set sail for home with the treasure. The three pirates are left on the island.

The next morning we fell early to work. Gray and Ben Gunn came and went with the boat while the rest piled treasure on the beach.

I was kept busy packing the money into bags.

Day after day this work went on.

The third night, the wind brought us a noise.

The three pirates!

It was decided that we must desert them on the island. We left powder and shot, salt goat, medicines and some other necessities.

At last one fine morning we weighed anchor.

Coming through the narrows, we saw all three of them kneeling.

The Doctor told them of the stores we had left.

They continued to call us and appeal to us not to leave them to die. Seeing the ship still on her course, one sent a shot whistling over Silver's head.

They stop in South America to hire more men. Silver goes off with some of the gold. Jim tells us what happened to the other men.

We cast anchor in a beautiful land-locked gulf, met the Captain of an English man-of-war, went on board his ship and had so agreeable a time.

When we came alongside 'The Hispaniola' Ben Gunn was on deck. Silver was gone and so had one of the sacks of coin. We were all pleased to **be so cheaply quit of him**.

We got a few hands and reached Bristol.

be so cheaply quit of him – get rid of him so easily

All of us had an ample share of the treasure. Captain Smollett is now retired. Gray saved his money. Ben Gunn was back begging. Of Silver we heard no more.

The silver and arms lie where Flint buried them. The worst dreams I have are when I hear the surf booming or start upright in bed with the sharp voice of Captain Flint, 'Pieces of eight! Pieces of eight!'

THE END